AIRCRAFT

Stealth Fighters and Bombers

Don Berliner

Enslow Publishers, Inc.

40 Industrial Road	PO Box 38
Box 398	Aldershot
Berkeley Heights, NJ 07922	Hants GU12 6BP
USA	UK

http://www.enslow.com

Library of Congress Cataloging-in-Publication Data

Berliner, Don.
  Stealth fighters and bombers / Don Berliner.
    p. cm. — (Aircraft)
Includes bibliographical references (p.   ) and index.
  ISBN 0-7660-1567-X
  1. Stealth aircraft—United States—Juvenile literature. [1. Stealth aircraft.
2. Bombers. 3. Airplanes, Military.] I. Title. II. Aircraft (Berkeley Heights, NJ)
  UG1242.S73 B47 2001
  623.7'463—dc21
                                        00-010049

Printed in the United States of America

10 9 8 7 6 5 4 3 2 1

To Our Readers: All Internet Addresses in this book were active and appropriate when we went to press. Any comments or suggestions can be sent by e-mail to Comments@enslow.com or to the address on the back cover.

Photo Credits: © Corel Corporation, pp. 11, 18, 31, 41; Department of Defense, p. 26; Robert F. Dorr, pp. 27, 29; Lockheed Martin Skunk Works, pp. 14, 17, 24; Northrop Corporation, p. 34; U.S. Air Force, pp. 4–5, 7, 9, 12, 15, 20, 21, 23, 30, 32, 36, 38, 39.

Cover Photo: U.S. Air Force, Courtesy of Robert F. Dorr

Contents

CHAPTER 1

Stealth in Action

F-117A Stealth Fighters

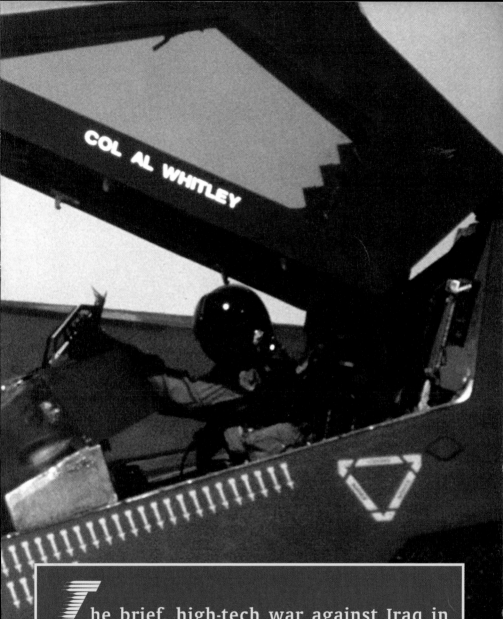

The brief, high-tech war against Iraq in 1991—Operation Desert Storm—saw a lot of new ideas become reality. The most unusual, and the most successful, of these ideas was the stealth fighter. It utilized the most advanced technology to carry out attacks using the "invisible" F-117A Nighthawk stealth fighters.

Everyone in the military forces knew that Baghdad, the ancient capital of Iraq, was the most heavily defended city in the world. It had thousands of antiaircraft guns and guided missile launchers ready to shoot down enemy aircraft. All the defenses were controlled by radar, which uses radio beams to find aircraft and other objects at night and in bad weather. The radio beams send information about the aircraft's location, altitude, and speed to the antiaircraft weapons. The weapons zero in on the attacking aircraft and shoot them down.[1]

If U.S. air attacks on Baghdad were to be carried out successfully and safely, something had to be done to knock out the guns and missiles before they could be fired. Even better, something had to be done to keep the ground radar from finding the attacking airplanes.

That is where the F-117As came in. Other types of fighters and bombers show up on radar as big, bright spots called blips. That makes them easy to track and easy to target. But the F-117A is a stealth fighter. It shows up on the radar screen as a tiny blip that could be a bird or even static. It is as though the F-117A is not there at all.

≡ Stealths over Baghdad

It is January 17, 1991. Many of the fifty or so F-117As based in Saudi Arabia are sent out as the first wave of the attacking force. Their mission is to drop guided bombs on

F-117A stealth fighter aircraft line the runway prior to takeoff.

the most important targets and then streak back to their home base before the Iraqis realize what is happening.

If the United States is able to knock out the main communications centers that control the Iraqi antiaircraft system, U.S. bombers and fighters that follow can operate in relative safety. It is one of the most important missions in this or any war. The success of the entire attack depends on a few pilots and their very special new airplanes.

As they approach Baghdad, the pilots can see a brightly lit city.[2] This is a good sign. If the Iraqis had picked up the F-117As on their radar, every light would have been turned off to keep their enemies guessing where the main targets were. The intense training before the mission has taught the pilots the locations of these important targets. Now they will not waste their bombs on buildings that will not play major roles in the war that is about to begin.

The Nighthawks streak over Baghdad at more than 600 miles per hour in darkness. People on the ground can hear them, but the planes fly so fast that by the time they are heard, they are gone. The pilots open the doors of their bomb bays in each airplane's belly. The guided bombs are launched, and the airplanes turn around and head home.

The bombs "know" where to go. A map of the target was loaded into each bomb before takeoff. The bombs have radar equipment in their noses that compares what the bomb is pointed at with the map. It is almost as

Stealth Fighters and Bombers

Pilot Major Joe Bowley sits in the cockpit of this F-117A stealth fighter aircraft. He is getting ready for the flight home after Operation Desert Storm.

though there is a pilot in each bomb who steers it toward its target.[3] The bombs plunge down, each toward its selected target. Some follow their orders so precisely that they fly into the correct window in a building and blow up vital equipment before it can even be turned on.

The Iraqis know they are being attacked, and attacked very successfully. But they cannot see the attacking airplanes or find them on their radar. It is as though the attacker's airplanes are ghosts. The Iraqis are helpless as one important building after another is blasted.

After just a few F-117As attack, the Iraqi military machine is blind and crippled.[4] The Iraqis may not realize it, but this modern way of fighting war is saving hundreds or even thousands of lives. If the attack were being carried out the old-fashioned way, with bombers dropping hundreds of tons of bombs over the entire city, many civilians would have been killed or injured. But this attack is carried out with the precision of a surgeon removing a patient's tonsils.

The F-117As are flown back to the base, where everyone is waiting to hear the outcome of history's first mass attack by stealth airplanes. Even before the radar photos taken from airplanes flying high over Baghdad have been processed, it is clear that the attack was a great success. The Iraqi radar control system is in ruins. The country's telephone system barely works. The guided bombs have done their jobs, and few people have suffered.[5]

As for the F-117As and their pilots, none suffers a single sign of damage. There is not one bullet hole in an F-117A, let alone a dent or a scratch.[6] Hundreds of millions of dollars spent to create these airplanes has paid off.

CHAPTER 2

What Is Stealth?

*S*tealth means "sneaky." It also indicates a high-tech way of fooling radar. Radar was made practical before World War II by English scientists and engineers. They were testing some equipment near the coast when their radio waves were reflected by ships at a distance. By the time the war started, they had built a string of radar stations along the coast opposite France. From there, they could detect fleets of German fighters and bombers when they were still far away. This gave them time to launch their own fighters to attack the Germans.

The Germans built their own radar, helping them track the Allies' huge fleets of bombers that were attacking German war

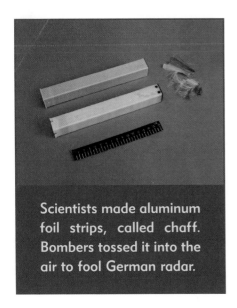

Scientists made aluminum foil strips, called chaff. Bombers tossed it into the air to fool German radar.

plants. To fool radar, scientists produced something called chaff. Chaff was nothing more than thin strips of aluminum foil, like the tinsel that decorates Christmas trees. A lot of chaff was tossed out of bombers as they approached their targets. The German radar picked up the chaff and thought each piece might be a small airplane. It wasted a lot of their ammunition and worked well enough to fool them for a while.

The Germans changed their radar so that it would not be fooled so easily by chaff. The Allies then changed the chaff. It went back and forth, with first the Allies ahead, and then the Germans. But few people at that time thought of making airplanes less visible to radar.[1]

When an aircraft such as the F-117A fighter contains stealth devices, radar will see it as something smaller than a sparrow. To the kind of radar that points antiaircraft guns, it does not look like an airplane or show up large enough to lock onto for firing. The guns do not know where to point. They have to be aimed by hand, and this is too slow to follow 600-mile-per-hour F-117As.

Many stealth techniques are still very secret, because if enemies knew how they were being fooled, they might be able to figure out a way to fool stealth in return. However, even some civilians have a pretty good idea about how some stealth techniques work.

The Secret Stealth

The F-117A fighter is one aircraft with stealth devices. The most obvious stealth idea built into the F-117A Nighthawk is its peculiar shape. Every other type of airplane has lots of curves to make it more streamlined, so the air will flow around it smoothly. In particular, the tops of the wings are rounded to allow the airplanes to fly faster, farther, and higher. But lots of curves can make an airplane show up big on radar.

The F-117A does not have a single curve. Instead, it has numerous flat plates. At first glance, it looks as though it should not be able to fly. In fact, it can fly only if some amazingly complicated electronic systems are working. If these systems fail, the pilot has to punch out: He must use his ejection seat to shoot himself out of the cockpit. His parachute will then open to let him down gently.

Why build an airplane with such an odd shape if it causes such problems? The many flat sides of the F-117A are designed to deflect radar waves and keep them from reflecting back to the enemy's equipment. With absolutely flat surfaces, called skin panels, facing in dozens of different directions, the radar waves will bounce off in just as many directions. Very few of the waves will find their way back to the enemy's radar

The F-117A stealth fighter has no curves. The flat sides deflect radar waves, making the plane "invisible."

transmitter, whether on the ground or in an airplane. The radar will keep hunting for things it cannot spot.

The entire outside of a stealth airplane is painted flat black, which will not reflect sunlight like light colors or shiny paint. More importantly, this paint is radar absorbent. The process is still secret, but the paint may consist of two layers. The outside layer lets the radar waves in. The inside layer then reflects them, but the outside layer will not let them back out. The waves bounce back and forth between the two layers of paint until they die out.[2]

The stealth airplane and its paint must be in perfect condition if they are to work. Just a little dent or scratch in the airplane's skin will reflect the radar and could reveal the airplane's location. If the paint has been chipped, it will reflect the radar as well. This means the airplane's ground crew has to keep it in near perfect condition.

Inside Stealth

Inside the stealth airplane, there are black boxes—electronic devices that make it hard to track the airplane. A black box can change the reflected radar wave before it

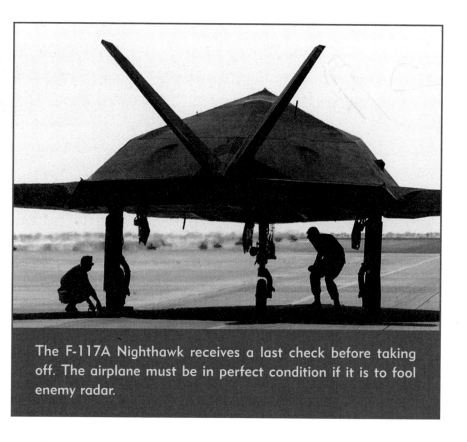

The F-117A Nighthawk receives a last check before taking off. The airplane must be in perfect condition if it is to fool enemy radar.

travels back to the ground. This can make it seem as though the stealth airplane is in another place. A black box may also change the frequency of the reflected radar waves so that the enemy's radar set will not recognize them.

In addition to these two black-box techniques, there are many new ideas used in the newest stealth airplanes. And there are rumors of a lot of other ideas that are still being tested. There is a constant battle between the radar engineers who try to detect stealth aircraft and the stealth engineers who design the aircraft.

Specifications for
F-117A Nighthawk

Length—65 feet 11 inches

Height—12 feet 5 inches

Wingspan—43 feet 4 inches

Wing area—1,140 square feet

Fuel—Jet fuel (high-grade kerosene)

Maximum speed—650 miles per hour

Cruising speed—600+ miles per hour

Rate of climb—Classified

Maximum altitude—Classified

Crew—1 pilot

Endurance—Classified

Range on internal fuel tanks—1,000 miles; can be refueled in air

Engines—2 General Electric F404 turbofans, rated at 10,800 pounds of thrust each

Empty weight—29,500 pounds

Gross weight (maximum weight with fuel and crew)—52,500 pounds

CHAPTER 3

Stealth Airplanes

The first truly stealthy airplane to enter service was Lockheed's F-117A Nighthawk, a fighter-bomber. It has no guns or missiles to attack other airplanes, but it does carry bombs. Everything about it is meant to make it hard to track on radar. As a result, it is one of the oddest-looking airplanes ever to fly. But there are very good reasons it looks the way it does.

The F-117A is about 66 feet long, and its wingspan is over 43 feet. It is 12 feet 5 inches tall when parked on the ground. Its wings are swept back 67 degrees, which is the most of any American airplane. When it is empty, it weighs about 30,000 pounds.

When it is full of fuel and weapons, it may weigh as much as 52,500 pounds.

The F-117A: Power and Speed

The Nighthawk is powered by two very advanced turbojet engines. Each engine produces almost 11,000 pounds of thrust. This is equal to almost 20,000 horsepower each when the airplane is flying at its top speed. This compares with 100 to 200 horsepower for a family car, and 300,000 horsepower for a large airliner. Even without refueling in flight, an F-117A can fly about 1,000 miles. It can be refueled in flight by tanker planes. It can also carry an extra fuel tank in its weapons bay, in the bottom of the airplane. This way, it can make long flights when it is not in combat. The top speed of the F-117A is still a secret, but most experts think it is between 600 and 650 miles per hour. The airplane lands at more than 170 miles per hour, which is so fast it has to use a parachute to help it stop on short runways.[1]

The only markings the F-117A carries are several U.S. Air Force insignias in light gray and its squadron emblem. The pilot's name is painted just below his side window. Even the inside of the cockpit is painted black to cut down on reflections. The windows are made of quartz and coated with gold so that they will not reflect radar.

Most of the airplane is made of ordinary aluminum. The doors of the weapons bay and the landing gear are made of advanced materials such as carbon fiber. The exhaust pipes from the engines are made of nickel alloy in

The wingspan of the F-117A is more than 43 feet.

On short runways, the F-117A needs a parachute to help it stop.

a honeycomb shape. The rudders (vertical tails) are made from advanced graphite composite materials. These special (and very expensive) materials absorb radar waves and help make the F-117A hard to track.

F-117A Equipment

Most of the equipment an F-117A carries is secret. But it is known that it has infrared detectors that can locate other airplanes or missiles by the heat they put out. The F-117A has the most advanced navigation devices, including the Global Positioning System (GPS). The GPS uses data from several satellites to give the pilot his exact location even at night or in thick clouds. The location appears on a color monitor in the cockpit. The monitor can be used for navigation or to help a pilot locate enemy airplanes and antiaircraft guns. It can also show him exactly how his engine is running.[2]

When an F-117A is on a combat mission, everything is hidden inside. The load of bombs or other weapons are carried in the weapons bay. Radio antennas are retracted like those on some cars. The doors of the weapons bay and the landing gear fit so well into the body of the plane that it is hard to see them. Anything that sticks out could be picked up by radar and give away the airplane's location.

The F-117A is shaped to be stealthy, and that makes it very hard to fly. The only way it can be controlled is with electronic black boxes. They compute what the pilot wants the airplane to do, and then send signals to the airplane so that it will fly the way it should. If the electronic black boxes were to stop working, the airplane would be impossible to control. The pilot would then have to pull a special handle to shoot his seat out of the cockpit. He would automatically be separated from the seat, and a parachute would lower him gently to the ground.

Hiding the Heat

It is not good enough to make an airplane invisible to just radar. Some detection systems can track infrared radiation that comes from anything that is hot. Very hot burned fuel-air mixture roars out of the tailpipe of every jet. If an enemy fighter had missiles that could track an

The F-117A stealth is refueled in midair by a KC-10 aerial tanker.

airplane by its infrared waves, it could shoot it down even if the pilot and his radar could not see it. Therefore, it is important for a stealth plane's heated exhaust to be concealed.

When an airliner flies at high altitude, it often leaves a white condensation trail, or contrail. This is caused by the heat from its exhaust condensing when it hits the cold air. The exhaust acts just like your breath on a cold day. Contrails are another giveaway to an airplane's location.

To reduce the heat coming out of the exhaust, cool air can be added to the exhaust of a stealth plane. The usually round exhaust pipes can be flattened and then

Scoops on the front of the plane take in air for the engine to mix with fuel and also help to cool the engine. They are shielded by a grid.

pointed slightly upward. They can have shields below them to help hide the exhaust until it can cool down. There is a lot of heat at the front of a jet engine, too. The big scoops that take in air for the F-117A engine are shielded by a grid that looks something like the insert in an old-fashioned ice-cube tray.[3]

There is yet another type of emission that can be tracked. This is the electronic waves that come from the airplane's radios and radar and navigation devices. Much of this radiation can be shielded. Types that cannot be shielded must be turned off, or at least turned down, when there is fear that they could be detected by the enemy.

Two ways that an airplane cannot be made undetectable are visually and aurally (by sound). A stealth airplane can be seen as easily in the daylight as any other kind of airplane. When they take part in air shows, stealth airplanes can be photographed as easily as any other kind. Certain colors of paint can make the plane a little harder to see in the daytime. At night, all its lights can be turned off, as long as there is no chance that other airplanes will run into it.

The other way a stealth airplane is just like other airplanes is its sound. The noise of the exhaust can be deadened a little by careful design of the exhaust pipes. But this can interfere with other stealth needs. A stealth airplane can fly high, so its noise does not sound so loud to people on the ground. But it may have to fly low in order to complete its mission. Engineers and scientists continue to try to find ways to make stealth aircraft quieter and harder to see.

B-2 Spirit

The F-117A is probably the only stealth airplane that will ever be made entirely of flat plates. When it was designed in the late 1970s, computers were not powerful enough to figure out how to shape a stealth airplane with curves. By the time the B-2 bomber was designed in the mid-1980s, more powerful computers were available. The B-2 has graceful, aerodynamic curves and is still very stealthy.

The B-2 stealth bomber was designed in the 1980s. It is a flying wing, without a body or a tail.

A bomber is a large airplane that carries bombs and missiles. It is used to destroy enemy targets only on the ground.

The B-2 stealth bomber is a flying wing. It has no fuselage (body) and no tail. It is simply a broad wing with everything fitted inside. In its huge bomb bays it can carry up to 40,000 pounds of guided bombs or cruise missiles. It can fly more than 5,000 miles before it needs to refuel. It can cruise at well over 500 miles per hour, as high as 50,000 feet.

The B-2 has much more advanced and much more secret stealth systems than the F-117A. It is made mainly

Specifications for B-2 Stealth Bomber

Length—69 feet

Height—17 feet

Wingspan—172 feet

Wing area—5,140 square feet

Fuel—Jet fuel (high-grade kerosene)

Maximum speed—650–700 miles per hour

Cruising speed—Classified

Rate of climb—Classified

Maximum altitude—50,000 feet

Crew—2 pilots

Endurance—Approximately 8 hours without air-to-air refueling

Range on internal fuel tanks—Over 5,000 miles without air-to-air refueling

Engines—4 General Electric F-118-GE-100 turbofans, rated at 19,000 pounds of thrust each

Empty weight—100,000 pounds

Gross weight (maximum weight with fuel and crew)—400,000 pounds

from high-tech materials such as graphite-epoxy. These materials are stronger than aircraft aluminum and lighter than steel. They absorb radar waves, making the B-2 very hard to track.

B-2s were first used in combat during the war in Kosovo in 1998. The B-2s flew nonstop all the way from Whiteman Air Force Base in Missouri to Kosovo. They dropped their bombs, often through thick clouds. Then they flew home without ever landing in Europe. This was made possible by refueling in flight from flying tankers.

Only fourteen B-2s have been built because they are so expensive. Each one costs between $1 billion and

$2 billion. They are used by the 509th Bomb Group at Whiteman Air Force Base. If the United States happens to get into a large war, these bombers will have to share the skies with much older bombers that are not stealthy. The B-2s will be used to attack the most heavily defended targets.[4]

F-22 Raptor

As soon as the F-117A stealth fighter showed how well it worked, the Air Force decided it needed a stealth fighter that was extremely fast. The same technology that made the curvy B-2 possible was used to design the first supersonic stealth fighter. *Supersonic* means "faster than the speed of sound," which is about 750 miles per hour at sea level and 650 miles per hour at high altitude, where the air is thinner. The new F-22 does not look anything like the F-117A. It has smooth curves everywhere, and its wings are diamond-shaped, instead of being swept back like the F-117A's.

The F-22 is a true fighter plane, not a fighter-bomber like the F-117A. It carries at least two kinds of air-to-air missiles for attacking other airplanes. It also has a 20-mm cannon that can be used to shoot down other airplanes or to attack ground targets, such as tanks or missile sites.

The F-22 uses much more advanced stealth systems than the F-117A. Because they are so new, they are very secret. The F-22 could be an important fighter plane for the U.S. Air Force for many years.[5]

The first supersonic stealth fighter, the F-22 Raptor, travels faster than the speed of sound. It carries missiles and a cannon to shoot down enemy planes or attack targets on the ground.

Specifications for
F-22 Raptor

Length—62 feet 1 inch

Height—16 feet 5 inches

Wingspan—44 feet 6 inches

Wing area—740 square feet

Fuel—Jet fuel (high-grade kerosene)

Maximum speed—Mach 2.5, or more than 1,600 miles per hour

Cruising speed— Approximately 1,000 miles per hour

Rate of climb—Classified

Maximum altitude— 66,000 feet

Crew—1 pilot

Endurance—Classified

Range on internal fuel tanks—Classified

Engines—2 Pratt & Whitney F119-PW-100 turbofans, rated at 35,000 pounds of thrust each

Empty weight—Over 30,000 pounds

Gross weight (maximum weight with fuel and crew)—Over 60,000 pounds

CHAPTER 4

The Stealth Pilot

Stealth airplanes are so different from other airplanes that you would think their pilots would have to be different, too. It seems as though stealth airplanes would be a lot different to fly. But that is just not the case.

Major Jeff Kindley is a B-2 pilot who was among the first to fly the big stealth bombers in combat. Each of his missions lasted thirty hours. In 1998, he and a second pilot flew from their air base in Missouri to Kosovo, in what used to be Yugoslavia. They dropped their bombs and flew home. They refueled in midair at least twice during the round-trip of more than 10,000 miles.

During a thirty-hour mission, the B-2 needs to be refueled in midair. This KC-10A pilot makes contact with the B-2 during flight, so that refueling can take place.

How did Jeff Kindley, a U.S. Air Force major, get to be picked to become a pilot of the world's most advanced bomber? "I was lucky, I guess," he said modestly.[1] He went through the standard U.S. Air Force flight training and then was trained to fly much older B-52 Stratofortress jet bombers. He also instructed student pilots in T-38 Talon jet trainers.

"Everybody [who was interested] turned in an application. Each base commander was allowed to pick two guys. Then we came to Whiteman [Air Force Base] for about a week. And we had to go through a competition."

≡ Simulator Training

During the competition at Whiteman, Major Kindley got to "fly" in a B-2 simulator. Using simulators is a safe yet realistic way to train pilots in the many steps necessary to fly a B-2. Using the B-2 simulator is like playing a video game. The inside looks like the inside of the plane, with all the flight controls. The pilot "flies" the bomber on a large screen. The simulator can throw many problems at the student to test his or her level of knowledge. It gives the student important practice in how to react to malfunctioning systems and to in-flight emergencies.

The main part of the simulator is a B-2 cockpit, with all the instruments and controls. Attached to the simulator is a lot of equipment that allows the entire simulator to move up and down and to tilt from side to side. This makes the pilot feel as though he is really flying the airplane. It is a more complicated and much more expensive version of the simulators used in automobile driving classes.

The view through the windshield is exactly like it would be from a real airplane; however, it is really just images projected on large computer screens. It shows scenery and sky when the simulator is "flying" at high altitude. When the student pilot is practicing landings, the view is of the airport. When the simulator "lands," the pilot feels a bump and hears the tires squeak as they "touch" the runway.

A simulator may cost as much as a real airplane. But it can be "flown" twenty-four hours a day. If the student

The B-2 cockpit has many instruments and controls. Pilots practice flying the bomber in a simulator like this one.

makes a big mistake and "crashes" the simulator, no airplane gets wrecked. More important, the pilot does not get hurt. The student can practice flying in bad weather even when the sun is shining. He can be trained to deal with emergencies that would be almost impossible to fly through.

Once Kindley showed his instructor how well he could "fly" the B-2 simulator, he was interviewed by a one-star general. He passed that interview, then went to a second. This was with a four-star general, the commander of air combat command. He was the top officer of all the fighter and bomber squadrons in the Air Force.

Just twenty experienced pilots were chosen from the applicants to be in the first B-2 squadron. All had been either fighter or bomber pilots for many years. Now they would learn how to be stealth bomber pilots. They spent six months learning all about the B-2. There were many hours spent in the classroom. They also spent 150 hours "flying" the B-2 simulator.

Finally, they got to fly the real airplane. After fifty hours at the controls of B-2s, the students were made part of the active squadron.

Flying the B-2 Bomber

There are all kinds of moving surfaces on the rear edges of the B-2's wings. These surfaces make the airplane turn right and left. Other surfaces act as the elevators, which make the plane point up and down, and the ailerons, which make it bank or tilt from side to side.

It would be a very complicated and difficult airplane to fly if it were not for all the computers. The pilot moves his controls the same way he would in any other airplane. Turning the control wheel like a car's steering wheel makes the airplane tilt to the side. Pushing the wheel forward makes the airplane tilt down, and pulling it back makes the airplane tilt up. Two pedals on the floor are used to make the airplane turn right and left. As the pilot maneuvers, the computers tell the controls on the wings what to do. One control surface may go up a little and

Without the many onboard computers, the B-2 would be very hard to fly. Here, the bomber sits in front of its hangar.

another down a lot. This would make the airplane turn and bank at the same time.

Major Kindley explained things from the pilot's point of view. "As far as what a pilot would do with his hands and feet, it's the same. Because it is computer controlled, it is an easy airplane to fly. The hardest part is learning how to master the computers. The newer airplanes have so much technology, and the pilot gets a tremendous amount of information. There are probably a hundred things to get used to."

After he learned how to fly the B-2 in all kinds of situations and all kinds of weather, it was time to prepare for flying it in combat.

≡ Ready for Combat

"About a week prior to each mission, you would study your mission plans every night," said Kindley. "You'd go to the briefings with the guys flying the missions before you." It is possible to put an entire mission plan into the simulator so that the pilots can "fly" the mission while they are still at their home base.

"Then the night before you fly, you come in and get briefed for your specific target area. We would show up about five hours prior to the flight," Kindley explained. "We would fly for about thirteen hours over there, about an hour and a half 'in country' as we call it, and thirteen hours back."

Was he at the controls for almost thirty hours, or did he have a relief crew? "We have two pilots. One is the pilot in command, and the other pilot is the mission commander." The mission commander deals with the weapons. "During cruising periods, one pilot will get out of his seat and stretch out in the back and take a nap." Although there is not a big area to sleep in, pilots stretch out either on the floor or right behind the seat.

"We bring a lawn chair. Air Force airplanes are not built for crew comfort. There's one spot [where] you can stand up, and that's it." It may seem surprising that an airplane costing as much as $2 billion does not even have a bed for one of the pilots, but it has to be so streamlined that there is not room.

Once the B-2 gets over enemy territory, it becomes very important that all its stealth systems work. If they do, the airplane and its crew will be safe. If they do not, the plane could be shot down.

"We have a lot of confidence in the B-2 the whole time," Major Kindley said. And then he admitted, "Certainly, there's a feeling you can't help the first time you do that to be a little nervous and to be afraid [it might not] work like it's supposed to. On my first mission I didn't sleep very much. But it did work great. When the airplane had not flown in combat everybody *hoped* it

Pilots are briefed before their mission.

A B-2 bomber aircraft prepares for its first flight at the Air Force Flight Test Center.

would do well. And now that it has, the confidence level of everybody that was involved with it has gone up."

Even if the enemy cannot track the B-2s on radar, it can hear them. The enemy knows there are airplanes up in the sky that are dropping bombs and blowing up their airfields and buildings. The antiaircraft guns fire in the general direction of the sounds, as do the surface-to-air missiles.

"You see the tracers [cannon shells that light up so that the gunners can see where the shells are going]. You can see the antiaircraft fire that's being shot at other airplanes that are in the sky at the same time." Many shells and missiles were fired at Major Kindley and his fellow pilots. But not a single one of them was hit. It was as though the B-2 had a shield around it.

Once the Kosovo command and control centers were knocked out of action, there was no way for the Serbians to control their antiaircraft fire. "When we were trying to stop [Serbian dictator Slobodan] Milosevic's army, we started striking petroleum storage fields." They blasted a lot of those fields to pieces. Without gasoline and diesel fuel, the army's tanks and trucks came to a stop.

Major Kindley thought carefully about the future of stealth. "I think stealth is going to be around for a while. There are people out there that say they have equipment that can track stealth airplanes. I'm sure there are things out there, but it would be hard for every country to . . . track stealth airplanes. They're not invisible, but they're very hard to see. They're very hard to shoot at. A lot of things have to happen for the [enemy] to be able to track us, guide on us, and shoot us."

CHAPTER 5

The Future of Stealth

I t is hard to imagine that the United States would build future bombers and fighters that are not built with stealth in mind. As radar, infrared, and other detection devices get better, the stealthiness of airplanes must also improve. It is not clear if this will lead to more airplanes with strange shapes like the B-2 flying wing bomber or if it will lead to even better airplanes with more ordinary shapes, like the F-22.

More than likely, stealth technology will show up on more kinds of weapons. Already, cruise missiles are becoming stealthy. The most advanced helicopters have stealth shapes and probably stealth systems inside. Unmanned drone airplanes that are used to take television pictures of battlefields will also use stealth to keep them safe. Even naval ships can make use of stealth to defend themselves against missiles and torpedoes.[1]

There are much more advanced airplanes that are still very, very secret. For years there have been reports in aviation magazines of super-fast airplanes that have been tracked at Mach 6 (4,000 miles per hour) or faster over wide-open areas of Nevada. This kind of speed was achieved as long ago as 1961 by the rocket-powered X-15 research airplanes, so scientists know how to make airplanes fly that fast. Future combat and spy planes will have to be stealthy to keep them safe from enemy radar and missiles.

Stealth is here to stay. From now on, airplanes, helicopters, and cruise missiles that fly into dangerous skies will have to be stealthy. One day it may even be possible to make airplanes almost invisible to the naked eye, and silent as well.

Chapter Notes

Chapter 1. Stealth in Action

1. Norman Friedman, *Desert Victory: The War for Kuwait* (Annapolis, Md.: The Naval Institute Press, 1992), pp. 148–149.

2. D.M. Giangreco, *Stealth Fighter Pilot* (Osceola, Wis.: Motorbooks International, 1993), p. 95.

3. Friedman, pp. 184–185.

4. Giangreco, p. 98.

5. Friedman, p. 147.

6. Giangreco, p. 100.

Chapter 2. What Is Stealth?

1. *The American Heritage History of Flight* (American Heritage Publishing Co., 1962), p. 290.

2. Dennis R. Jenkins, *Lockheed Martin F-117 Nighthawk* (North Branch, Minn.: Specialty Press, 1999), p. 69.

Chapter 3. Stealth Airplanes

1. Mark Lambert, ed., *Jane's All the World's Aircraft* (London: Jane's Information Group, 1992), p. 404.

2. Ibid., pp. 403–404.

3. Dennis R. Jenkins, *Lockheed Martin F-117 Nighthawk* (North Branch, Minn.: Specialty Press, 1999), p. 72.

4. Lambert, pp. 426–427.

5. Steve Pace, *Lockheed Skunk Works* (Osceola, Wis.: Motorbooks International, 1992), pp. 175–182.

Chapter 4. The Stealth Pilot

1. All dialogue in this chapter is from a telephone interview with U.S. Air Force Major Jeff Kindley, March 9, 2000.

Chapter 5. The Future of Stealth

1. Richard Aboulafia, *Heavy Bombers, End of an Era?* January 12, 1998, vol. 148, p. 18.

aileron—A movable panel on the back of an airplane wing, used to make the airplane bank or roll.

air-to-air missile—A missile shot from one airplane at another airplane in flight.

air-to-surface missile—A missile shot from an airplane toward a target on the ground.

antiaircraft gun—Cannon that shoots at attacking airplanes.

bomber—A large airplane that carries bombs and missiles. It is used to destroy enemy targets only on the ground.

composite materials—Materials made of two or more different materials that have superior strength or other advanced properties.

endurance—The length of time an airplane can stay in the air without refueling.

fighter—One- and two-seat airplanes that carry guns and missiles. Most carry guns in their wings, and missiles are slung under the wings. Others, such as the F-117A Nighthawk and the F-22 Raptor, carry their missiles inside. The missiles are used to shoot down enemy airplanes and destroy enemy targets on the ground.

GPS—Global Positioning System. A system using satellites that pinpoints locations on Earth.

guided bomb—A bomb dropped by an airplane that can change its direction using built-in radar to search for its target.

honeycomb—A strong lightweight structure made of connected cells.

infrared—The wavelength of radiation situated outside the visible spectrum of light, past the red end.

Mach Number—The ratio of the speed of an object to the speed of sound (about 650 miles per hour at high altitude, 750 miles per hour at sea level). Mach 1 is equal to the speed of sound; Mach 2 is twice as fast.

radar—Radio detecting and ranging. A system that transmits radio waves and processes their reflections for display, showing an object's shape, location, and velocity.

simulator—A device that allows a pilot to experience conditions that are likely to occur in actual flight.

stealth—Technology that incorporates different ways of hiding an aircraft from detection.

surface-to-air missile—A missile shot from the ground at an aircraft.

throttle—A device that controls the amount of fuel flowing into an engine, and thereby controls the speed of the craft.

weapons bay—A compartment in which bombs or missiles are carried.

Further Reading

Goodall, James C. *America's Stealth Fighters and Bombers*. Osceola, WI: MBI Publishing Co., 1997.

———. *F-117A Stealth in Action*. Carrollton, TX: Squadron Signal Publications, 1991.

Jenkins, Dennis R. *Lockheed Martin F-117 Nighthawk*. North Branch, MN: Specialty Press, 1999.

Lake, Jon. *Jane's How to Fly and Fight in the F-117A Stealth Fighter*, San Francisco, CA: Harper Collins, 1997.

Pace, Steve. *The F-117A Stealth Fighter*. New York: TAB Books, 1992.

Simonsen, Erik. *This Is Stealth: The F-117 and B-2—in Color*. Mechanicsburg, PA: Stackpole Books, 1992.

World's Greatest Stealth and Reconnaissance Aircraft. New York: Smithmark Publishers, 1991.

Internet Addresses

The Boeing Company. *Sea Launch*. "Military Airplanes."
©2000. <http://www.boeing.com/defense-space/
military> (December 12, 2000).

Lockheed Martin Aeronautics Company. *F-22 Raptor*.
"Historical Photos." November 7, 2000. <http://
www.lmasc.lmco.com/f22/rptwatch.htm> (December
12, 2000).

National Aeronautics and Space Administration. *Off to a
Flying Start*. "Introduction to Flight." December 27,
1999. <http://ltp.larc.nasa.gov/flyingstart/module1.
html> (December 12, 2000).

U.S. Air Force. "Fact sheet: F-117A Nighthawk." March
1996. <http://www.af.mil/news/factsheets/F_117A_
Nighthawk.html> (December 12, 2000).

Yahoo! Geocities. *American Fighters and Bombers*. n.d.
<http://www.geocities.com/CapeCanaveral/Hangar/
3314/> (December 12, 2000).

Index

8662